POETIC BLOOD RUNS DEEP

IN MEMORY OF MY MOTHER, LEONA MCCOY YOUNG

MARCH 1924 – MARCH 2019

She was the eldest of two girls, married after graduating high school
To my dad, Noah Young. Once married my parents joined the great
Migration from South Carolina going up to the North. First making
Residence in Washington D.C., for a brief period. Next and final stop
For my parents was Baltimore, Maryland. Noah and Leona raised nine
Children, five girls and four boys in the Cherryhill Community in
South Baltimore. Having a two-parent household had its advantages.
I have to say that my parents were kind and generous to all who crossed
Their paths. If I, George Young could do it all over again, I would not
Change a thing. Family Life was good, despite trials and tribulations,
We survived. Poetic Blood Runs deep is a dedication to my mother,
The Poet. I spent many days and nights listening to her recite her
Poems, she was trying for perfection. Often, I would add a word or two
to complete her poetry. Sharing her gift with the world is long overdue.
This compilation of her work along with my own will share a story
Of life. I promise once you, the reader picks it up, you will enjoy
a mother and son's journey through life. It has all the elements that
we all face in surviving God's creation.

TABLE OF CONTENTS

1. MAMA
2. TAKE A LOOK
3. IF I COULD SPEAK
4. MEMORIES
5. GIG IS UP
6. WHAT ARE YOU GOING TO DO?
7. PEOPLE
8. DON'T WAIT
9. WHO BUT THE LORD
10. LETTER TO GOD
11. FINDINGING MYSELF IN MY DARKEST HOUR
12. OUTCOME
13. FACES
14 BUS DRIVER
15. SOMETIMES
16. YES YOU CAN
17. BOARDING THE BUS
18. LOVING YOU
19. LOVE
20. COMPUTER
21. COLLEGE
22. I FEEL GOOD
23. A MOTHER'S PAIN
24. A MOTHER – MY SON
25. OUR BEGINNING
26. I AM DOING MY BEST
27. BISEXUAL
28. BLESS MY SOUL
29. SEPTEMBER
30. PLAYTIME
31. WE LAND IN PLACES LIKE THIS
32. PAIN
33. SNOW
34. LIGHTS ARE OFF
35. ME
36. IN THE COUNTRY
37. GRADUATION
38. FIGHTING MY DEMONS
39. DECISIONS
40. EVERYTHING IS WONDERFUL
41. BORN AGAIN
42. CLARITY
43. GREETINGS
44. IMAGINATION
45. GET UO STAY UP
46. HAPPY HEAVENLY BIRTHDAY
47. HAPPY VALENTINE DAY

48. BIRTHDAY CARD
49. RETIRING
50. MY VALENTINE
51. HAPPY BIRTHDAY
52. GOING TO WORK ANY OLE WAY
53. REMEMBER ME
54. FRIENDS
55. SCARS
56. THE PROGRAM
57. LOVE CONQUERS ALL
58. HOME
59. THINGS CHANGE
60. MY CHILD MY CHILD
61. GOD WILL COMFORT YOU
62. LOVE
63. THESE TWO EYES OF MINE
64. FIRE
65. I AM BLESSED
66. LOVE STORY
67. THE DARK CLOUDS ABOVE
68. LOVING YOU
69. TREE ROOTS
70. OLGA
71. SEASONS
72. GOOD EATING
73. CRY FOR HELP
74. I CRY FREEDOM
75. WAGERING A WAR AGAINST FATHER TIME
76. REFLECTIONS
77. FRIENDSHIP
78. FREEDOM TRAIN
79. OBITUARY

MAMA

Mama is the one who loves everyone

Mama is the one who gets things done

Mama is the one who says we must

Mama is the one with so much trust

Mama is the one with so much hope

Mama is the one who jumps rope

Mama is the one who sings like a dove

Mama is the one I really love

Written by Michelle Renee Moody

TAKE A LOOK

Look in the mirror, then look at me

Our aging faces is what you will see

One thing for sure, if we live long enough

We will have happy days and many that are rough

Our steps will be slower, our speech not so clear

Old age keeps creeping until it is here

Just try to remember your young days past

No need of wishing that they will last

Every good thing must end

Our youth we cannot extend

So, get that thought out of your mind

Sure, soon you will see the sign of graying hair

Wrinkles quite a few, in both you and me

So, do not be upset, take it in stride

Make those changes with dignity and pride

Written by Leona McCoy Young

HOWBEIT WHEN HE, THE SPIRIT OF TRUTH, IS COME, HE WILL GUIDE YOU INTO ALL TRUTH, FOR HE SHALL NOT SPEAK OF HIMSELF BUT WHATSOEVER HE SHALL HEAR, THAT SHALL HE SPEAK: AND HE WILL SHEW YOU THINGS TO COME

JOHN 16:13

IF I COULD SPEAK

If I failed to say goodbye

Or held your hand so tight

Never gave you reason

To believe I never see morning light

The dawning of early morning

Or the sun high in the sky

The light of God was shining

My heart was saying goodbye

Remember me as you wish

In your own distinct way

You knew I would soon leave you

In months, weeks, or any day

God gave me this breath of life

I lived it as I knew how

I was afraid of God

I have left you and gone to him now

It is not man duty to judge me

It was God who gave me life

He gave me blessings

Through pain, love fear and strife

Written by Leona McCoy Young

MEMORIES

Memories of past years

Thought of Mama bring me to tears

I miss those days

Love in the family, love in the air

Oh, Mama, I miss you I swear

Your words ring in my head

Son, go to school, be well read

Keep your head to the sky

Always open your eyes

Do not let life pass you by

Troubles will come, but they will not last long

They will just linger for a while

Have no regrets

Walk this life always being at your best

You are my son; I remember the day you were born

Memories of past years, they may bring you to tears

But my son you will overcome

Written by George Young

GIG IS UP

Holding on to what was

Not wanting to star trek my way into worm holes

Scared to take the next step, afraid to breathe my next breath

Voices in my head have speared my insecurities

I will admit that I am scared

Lions, Tigers and Bears, oh my

My thoughts are with Dorothy when she cried

There is no place like home

There were no cell phones, no one to call

Thinking back to my conversation with ET

I too was loss and all alone, I could not phone home

How do I face my biggest fears?

After all these years

Dancing with wolves was my claim to fame

Why now experience any shame?

In my life I walked through the lion's den

There has been sin after sin

When the gig is up

Shall I accept my fate

Recognizing that I was a dollar short and a day late

Shall I drop down to my knees

Screaming forgive me for all my bad deeds

Or should I open my eyes

To realize that the universe is pleased

That I shared life, love, and happiness

That is my true success

When the gig is up, it is up

Written by George Young

WHAT ARE YOU GOING TO DO?

After everything has been done and said

Witnessing the good with the bad

Tears at no notice are drip dropping from my head

Run Nigga run, is a thing of the past

Life is to be lived

This too shall pass

Sometimes, I just want to tell everyone, Kiss My Ass

I have suffered enough

Growing pains that forever remain

Haunted by my boogie man

I know that sounds insane

Treading through unfulfilled dreams

Witnessing landmine explosions

I've experienced every emotion

As of today

I have chosen

To shed my skin

Making that transformation from Caterpillar to Butterfly

Soaring high above the sky

Thrusting forward like John Henry

Moving fast like Speed Racer

Aware pf all potholes to avoid disaster

No more sharing duties with Atlas

From this point on, I will be wiser

Written by George Young

PEOPLE

I could write a book

About the people I see

All the time wondering

What do they think of me

About their woes and troubles

The young and the old

Life with sisters and brothers

In every person's life

There is sadness and joy

There is something that is shared

It may be a special toy

Life goes on and on

Until God calls us home

Remember in our sadness

We are never alone

Written by Leona McCoy Young

DON'T WAIT

Give me my flowers now

While I am alive

Let me see the beauty of flowers of many colors

Let smell their sweetness and enjoy the gift of others

Let the roses please me

Their beauty I can see

Give me with Love from the depths of your heart

Let the pansies make me smile

Give me flowers while I am alive

Don't wait until I close my eyes

Never to open them again

Never to see the beauty of roses, white yellow or red

Give me flowers while I can see

The beauty that God gave to you and me

Written by Leona McCoy Young

WHO BUT THE LORD

Who but the Lord

Through my pain and strife

Who but the Lord

Gave me a new life

He gave me strength and courage

Gave me faith, removed fear

Who but the Lord is the reason I am here

He gave to all compassion

To men and women alike

When I felt the weakest

He always picked up the slack

Who but the Lord

Made my life complete

Who but the Lord

Made me complete

Who but the Lord

Made me strong, not weak

Yes, he blessed my soul

I'll praise him in every way

For who but the Lord

Kept me from day to day

Written by Leona McCoy Young

LETTER TO GOD

You want to talk about loss

People leaving my life without notice

Not believing that happened, that they're gone

Feeling in my gut that rips my heart, my soul

Changing my outlook on life

Not having any power to save the ones you love

All the tears in the world cannot take back death

It's final, hurtful and downright devasting

It's a nightmare that I relive over and over as the years pass

Although we are destined to die

Death is an unforgettable act towards mankind

Dear God why?

Written by George Young

FINDING MYSELF IN MY DARKEST HOUR

Seeking a way out

Trapped in darkness

Same scene repeats itself

No matter how I do it

I get the same results

Why can't I just stop without a thought

One last time, it's my choice

Crying away my pain

Despair mixed with so much shame

I keep doing the same thing over and over again

I fear my end

My life was not supposed to be like this

I can't see straight, I can't think, it's like I don't exist

Finding myself in my darkest hour

I fear my end

Written by George Young

OUTCOME

My life changed on Edmondson and Pulaski streets

Waiting for an uber driver to take me to the airport

Not having any real thoughts

Second guessing myself

I just finished shooting dope

Veins busted, nose killing me

Shooting that needle in my ass was the only way

Seeking treatment was my way out of a miserable situation

That could set me free

Homeless and broke was not who or where I wanted to be

I finally surrendered to a power greater than myself

Known as my disease

Only then is when my life changed, drastically

Written by George Young

FACES

I recognized your face

I couldn't remember your name

I felt so ashamed

That's why I only said hello

I didn't talk with you more

Oh, how your children do grow

It seems that only a year ago

You were a little tot

Running and playing and crying a lot

Time does not wait

For anyone at all

You were steady growing

Getting very tall

With that growth

Your personality didn't change

That's what I remembered most

Before I remembered your name

Written by Leona McCoy Young

BUS DRIVER

We have our bus drivers

Both women and men

Before the school year ends

They have been so patient waiting for us

Loading and unloading from the bus

They drove us so carefully

To and From

When and wherever we wanted to go

Have a happy summer

Until the school year begins

So, you can drive us to places

Until the school year ends again

Written by Leona McCoy Young

SOMETIMES

I can bowl a hundred or more

Sometimes I bowl 99

Just can't get one more pin

Oh, this ball of mine

When I want it to go straight

It goes left or right

Leaving one pin standing

Rocking with all it's might

I'm hoping that it will fall

No, it's still there

Standing straight and tall

You know that's not fair

Now here in the tenth frame

I've got to concentrate to get every pin

To get three strikes this time

If I am to win

Written by Leona McCoy Young

YES, YOU CAN

You can succeed in life

Reach your highest goal

If you are sincere

Not just playing a role

You may shed some tears today

Laugh at yourself tomorrow

For things that didn't go well

For yourself you felt sorrow

For everyday will be different

From the previous day

Keep striving toward your goal

You're there before you know

Success in life is sweet

Failure in life is sad

Put your best foot forward

You will be so glad

Glad you didn't give up

Although the struggle was tough

Proud you kept on pushing

Even through it was sometimes rough

Written by Leona McCoy Young

BOARDING THE BUS

On my front porch I sat

Watching for the bus

Looking up the hill to see it

So, I wouldn't have to rush

Suddenly, I saw the bus coming around the curve

I started to run for it

At my age, I had the nerve

I couldn't help but laugh

As I ran to board the bus

My old legs aren't as strong as they use to be

Maybe the bus driver would wait a minute for me

Breathing hard as I arrived at the bus door

I had better stop doing this

I'm not young anymore

I have to give myself credit

I did fairly well

From the smile on people faces

Oh, yes, I could tell

Written by Leona McCoy Young

LOVING YOU

Honey loving you is wonderful

Loving you is so grand

I am proud to be your woman

Proud that you're my man

There may have been others

That you thought you loved

Loving me was made in Heaven above

Now our joys will be together

Our worries just one

Our life together has just begun

Honey loving you is so wonderful

Loving you is so grand

I am proud to be your woman

Proud that you are my man

Written by Leona McCoy Young

LOVE

Love to me is your wonderful smile

The closeness of you being near

Love is your joyful laugh

Love is your eyes so clear

It's easy to say I love you

Mean every word I say

Love is your easy going way

The sight of you

In the things you say and do

Written by Leona McCoy Young

COMPUTER

A letter came this morning

It was addressed to me

I opened it up and looked inside

It really was a great surprise

The bill inside had been paid

That's not what the letter read

My account was in arrears

When would I come in and pay

Send the money by mail

Or, would I rather go to jail

I had no intention of doing

I did think of suing

The bill had been paid

No other charges were made

Computer, computer, be more precise

Don't try to mess up my life

With unpaid bills charged to me

I have paid as you can see

Feed that computer right

My money is already tight

I pay my bills right on time

So, get that information in line

Written by Leona McCoy Young

COLLEGE

Maybe you didn't realize

I was always here

Standing close besides you

All because I care

I don't say it often

I love you very much

Study hard is what I said

Do the best you can

Set a goal to strive for

Rach out, grab my hand

I think of you in my prayers

Asking God to see you through

Trust in him and with your courage

I know he'll see you through

Written by Leona McCoy Young

I FEEL GOOD

They say life is better on life terms

Well, that took me a long time to learn

I had a past of self-inflicting harm

I would try this, try that

Never realizing that my actions were setbacks

Keeping me from short- and long-term goals

A path filled with unknowns

I didn't know that I would be broke and all alone

Self-esteem, self-respect would be gone

I now know that life is better on life terms

I feel good

Written by George Young

A MOTHER'S PAIN

Grief overwhelmed her, disbelief was her thoughts

Tragic end to a beautiful life

Not my son, I only got one

Her sorrows echoed into the heavens

God, why have you chosen my son?

I raised him from day one

To love unconditionally

To love everyone

No hate in his heart

He was smart, talented and thriving for success

Why now take him away, why all this mess?

I have to believe in the end

God knows best

My son may he rest in Paradise

Written by George Young

A MOTHER – MY SON

To the courthouse I had to go

Time went fast, not slow

Soon it was time for lunch

I hadn't even had brunch

The lawyer gave me a searching glance

As in wonder, If I were the parent

Of, the boy that sat across from me

Wondering what his fate would be

I myself believed in him

I felt he was telling the truth

How things happened on that day

When the authorities took him away

In his face I saw fear

In his eyes there was a tear

As slowly down his face it fell

Looking at him I could tell

That as he looked straight at me

The live I felt, he could see

Then a smile mixed with fear

As his name was called, I could hear

The steady beat of my heart

Lord how could I part?

From him so early in his life

To bear the pain, hurt and strife

All the years as his youth passed by

I felt that I would die

No, I had to live for him

The other children, yes for them

To let him know that I cared

Deep inside, how I feared

Years went by and then one day

My son came home to stay

He lived and loved for a short while

Then someone took his life away

This time, to stay

My other children, I love them all

As I loved him and can recall

That there was love, there was life

There was pain, and there was strife

Written by Leona McCoy Young

OUR BEGINNING

Look at us, we feel so proud

We could all scream out loud

Listen carefully while we tell

What we learned to do

We learned to read

We learned to write

Not at the same speed

When we first came here

Nine months ago

We made our letters

Very slow

We didn't know A from B

That one plus one was two

Now we know A to Z

We can count further than three

We thank our mother's and father's

We thank our teachers too

We feel so proud and happy

We thank you

Written by Leona McCoy Young

I AM DOING THE BEST

I am doing the best that I can

I am not the poorest of a poor man

I'll send you five and owe the rest

Don't try to put me to a test

To see if you can get more

I told you once that I was poor

I am doing the best that I can

Written by Leona McCoy Young

BISEXUAL

She does everything I want

I do love her with all my heart

She's beautiful like the sun rise

Pretty face, pretty eyes

I love the way she makes me feel

I'm experiencing something else that's just as real

I don't' know why I feel this way

This feeling, this desire

It lights my heart on fire

I hear what the people say

I hear what the people say

I hear the comments

Calling me gay

But,

He's the one I want

Written by George Young

BLESS MY SOUL

This life has taken its toll

Struggles are many

Life is not without envy

I screwed up

Over and over again

This life has made it hard to win

The fight is never ending

Mistakes are plenty

Heart filled with pity

Dreams squandered, many times I wandered

Not knowing what to do or where to go

Bless my soul

This life has taken its toll

I survived and I now thrive

Life is better than ever before

My mind craving success, I just want more

Life is good

I withstood my demons

Blessed my soul

Written by George Young

SEPTEMBER

Now that summer is over

Vacation has come to an end

September brings lots of things

That is when school begins

The ringing of the school bell

Let's you know you should be in line

To march into your classroom

Leave all play behind

If you will pay attention

To what your teacher says

You will gain more knowledge

That in later years will pay

Written by Leona McCoy Young

PLAYTIME

Oh, what a beautiful day

We can go outside and play

On the sliding board we'll slide

That's what children like to do

The merry go round is lots of fun

To make it turn, you can run

Around and push it fast or slow

With children saying go, go, go

Soon it is time to return back inside to rest

We'll take a nap

Then we will study for our test

Written by Leona McCoy Young

WE LAND IN PLACES LIKE THIS

Not by our wish

Beaten into surrender

Good times we can't remember

How did my life become a disaster?

Praying for relief

Not having faith in any beliefs

We land in places like this

Seeking relief from a pain that we tried to resist

Knowing my pain is self-inflicted by best

Out of control was my life

We land in places like this

Thank God that they exist

Redemption from the agony and pain

I now know that my actions were insane

I was caught up in this vicious game

Seeking drugs to relieve my pain

Crying out for God, even though I did not know his name

We land in places like this

It made me pissed

Change is a must for me to continue to exist

My soul to keep, my soul weeps

Shouting please help me get this

It's my only wish Written by George Young

PAIN

My heart is heavy with pain

I am burdened, I am sad

To watch you lying so still

It makes me feel bad

What can I do but pray

To our Heavenly Father above

Thanking him for you

Basking in his love

My faith, my desire, my hope

My belief in prayer

Even though I can't see Jesus

I know that he is there

Written by Leona McCoy Young

SNOW

So beautiful and so white

As it falls during the night

In every corner that can be found

Falling onto the ground

We can always play in the snow

It is lots fun

Your feet and hands get so cold

You fall when you try to run

We can make a snowman

We'll put a hat on his head

Buttons for his eyes

We'll paint his nose bright red

Written by Leona McCoy Young

THE LIGHTS ARE OFF

My music is playing

Lying on my back

I noticed a tear drop coming from my left eye

I am thinking, I am not sad

I have no reason to cry

I think good memories

Thinking of the past

I smile, I laugh

Why would I cry?

Afraid of the unknown

Visions of a better life

It scares me

I don't know why

There is a fire in me that burns for immortality

I know we all going to die

It seems that God has turned the lights back on

Written by George Young

ME

Some of these songs I hear on the air

Makes me wonder

How they got there

That is what made me pick up my pen and write

Just sit back and listen

Really relax

The poem you hear was written by me

Most of my friends call me Lee

I like to write poems

It gives me a thrill

There is no special time

At my own free will

I can be washing dishes or sweeping the floor

When the notion strikes me

I sweep no more

Written by Leona McCoy Young

IN THE COUNTRY

Down here in the country

Nowhere to go

First to the back

Then to the front door

Looking out across the field

All you see is grass

Trees so big they scare you

How did they grow so fast?

Roosters crowing early

Must be a quarter till four

I might as well get up

I won't be able to sleep anymore

The Hen has started cackling

Soon she will lay

There is a nest full of eggs

Each and every day

Written by Leona McCoy Young

GRADUATION

Finally made it

Step by step

Not by ourselves

With some help

Our mothers and fathers

They pushed us on

Encouraging our efforts

Kept us going strong

Many a rainy morning

We wanted to stay in bed

Mother called us and said get up sleepy head

Today is the day that we walk across the stage

Receiving a diploma, as we become of age

Congratulations

Written by Leona McCoy Young

FIGHTING MY DEMONS

Fighting my demons

I can't see straight

Days gone by, it's my life I hate

I am shooting up everyday

Wishing my life would just wash away

Help me lord

I can't stand the pain

Blood dripping from my veins is causing me to be insane

Looking for a way out of this game

I cry, spare me this pain

Fight my demons

I just want to remember my name

Set me free from all my misery

Help me Lord

I just want to be restored

Help me fight my demons

Written by George Young

DECISIONS

Decisions must be made

Life choices we never evade

Consequences of life can drive you mad

Knowing I failed makes me sad

My present situation

Where do I go from here?

I have it ask

Rock bottom going nowhere fast, I don't know how long I will last

Painful experience has kicked my ass

Today I grasp, asking for God's help is all that I ask

Spare me the pain

Spare me this life

There has been so much strife

Forgive me for all my failing task

I want to bask in the glory and make up for my past

I am sorry

I only ask

That you forgive me

Written by George Young

Everything is wonderful

Everything is fine

Be grateful, be thankful

For such love is divine

Your children love you

You they adore

Thank God for everything

Who could ask for me

Written by Leona McCoy Young

BORN AGAIN

I went outside in the chill and rain yesterday

First time in a long time, I felt no pain

No shivers, no shakes, and no aches

Oh, what a difference a day makes

I didn't need that wake-up blast

Thank God, I had to kiss no one's ass

No begging to start my day

No substance needed to get through

My mind was clear and free

My body was all me

I was living the right way

Taking suggestions and doing what they say

Sit, listen, don't pick up and pray

I have a reprieve from my addiction, its day by day

Written by George Young

CLARITY

Clarity is what I seek

Years of confusion, it reached its peak

I remember when I was young

Those days were filled with lots of fun

Being able to do this and that

I was sure that God had my back

Confusion has made its way into my life

Time after time, I was involved in a fight

Altercations were fought in my head

Somehow, I survived being amongst the dead

I finally figured it out

Life struggles, knowing what they were about

My mind cleared from my poisonous thoughts

Clarity has given me positive results

I now can see what clarity has given me

A brand-new start

Written by George Young

GREETING

The hugs and kisses

From relatives and friends

Just seeing each other

Bring smiles and grins

Such a relationship like ours

Has gone on for years

Bringing people together

Removing doubts and fears

If we can do this

There is so much we need

Through faith in God

We will succeed

God has kept us together

Our family miles apart

There is nothing like prayer

When it comes from the heart

Written by Leona McCoy Young

IMAGINATION

I would go out into the rain

Play with a toy boat

My neighbors may think, I am insane

Call the man in the little white coat

Then they would take me away

For no reason at all

Just my imagination went that day

To things past that I recall

Things that gave me pleasure

When I was a child

Things that I can treasure

Remember with a smile

Written by Leona McCoy Young

GET UP STAY UP

You are down right now

It doesn't have to be forever

Give yourself a chance

You can if you try

After one fall so low

You can't fall any further

Unless for yourself

You want a blanket or dirt for cover

That you can't feel

Whether it's hot or cold

Make that first step

Someone is standing by

If you stumble and fall

Get up any way

Give it all you've got

You might save yourself

From being in a cemetery lot

Written by Leona McCoy Young

HAPPY HEAVENLY BIRTHDAY

I remember this day because it's your birthday

Although you are not physically here

You are here in spirit

I will always honor the day of your birth

Without you, there is no me

Happy Birthday Mother, you will always be remembered

The love you provided, is love I still feel

I remember you Mother on your Special Day

Written by George Young

HAPPY VALENTINE DAY

As sure as the rain and sun

Makes the flowers grow

I love you my dear

I want you to know

I will love you always

I want you to be mine

To love forever

You're so lovely and sweet

It's love, true love

That makes my heart skip a beat

I've always loved you

I want you to be mine

Please say you will be my Sweet Valentine

Candy is sweet

Lemons are sour

My love for you

Gets sweeter every hour

I need you to be mine

Please say you will be

My Sweet Valentine

Written by Leona McCoy Young

BIRTHDAY CARD

Happy Birthday

I wish you joy and happiness on this special day

Enjoy to the fullest

In your own special way

Be grateful, be thankful

That this day arrived

Give thanks to God

That you are alive

Happy Birthday

Written by George Young

RETIRING

Here you have been so faithful

Patient and very kind

Giving of yourself

Never seeming to mind

Someone we could trust

Caring and full of love

You have been like a mother

You aren't retiring, your just leaving

To start all over again

Doing so many things

You don't know where to begin

Always yes and never no

Whenever a favor was asked

Nothing seemed too hard, not even a difficult task

We will miss your pleasant smile

We love you, we care

We respect you so much

You are so dear

Written by Leona McCoy Young

MY VALENTINE

Honey, I love you

With all my heart

Even for a moment

I hate for us to be apart

Always and forever

I want you to be mine

You're sweeter than honey

You are better than wine

I love you

Please be my Valentine

Written by Leona McCoy Young

HAPPY BIRTHDAY

You came to us years ago

From our Heavenly Father above

A very precious gift who gave us so much love

You've brought us so much happiness

Just glad that you survived

Our prayers were answered

You added joy to our lives

Happy Birthday

I pray that you have many more

I hope you have many blessings

That life has in store

Happy Birthday

You are loved

Written by Leona McCoy Young

GOING TO WORK ANY OLE WAY

I'm feeling kind of bad this morning

But that's okay

I'm going to work

Any ole way

My dress is the same one I wore two days ago

Lord, I hope the run in my stockings, don't show

Children come first

There is no doubt

I'm feeling kind of sick this morning

But I got to get out

School is going to open

The children need new clothes

Where all the money coming from

Only Heaven knows

My man up and left me

Quite a while back

Couldn't stand the pressure of being a man and black

I've got to raise these children

I don't have a man

The lord above knows

I'm doing the best I can

I'm feeling kind of bad this morning

That's okay, I'm going to work any ole way. Leona M Young pg.52

REMEMBER ME

If I die before I wake, I won't know that I am gone

But, you will

Just remember to sing my favorite songs

Tell my jokes that I once told

Play my videos, showing how we, all got along

If I die before I wake

Shed a tear or two

Even if it's fake

Make speeches telling my good deeds

Be convincing, make everyone believe

Protect my name

Knowing I was once good at playing the life game

If I die before I wake

Remember Me

Written by George Young

FRIENDS

Started out with many

Now, I just have frenemies

Sad as it may seem

I remember we all had dreams

Blood Brother Rituals we swore to

Only to forget that one plus one equals two

Together we promised to keep our friendship forever

As fate would have it

These Blood Brother Rituals

It didn't matter

Life has driven us to different roads

Some ending in dead ends

Yes, I've lost a lot of friends

I do remember the good times we shared

Friends are just memories of my past

I do have friends today

These friends are not from around the way

If only we could perform the Blood Brother Ritual

Just then, maybe my friends will be forever

Written by George Young

SCARS

Scars are life long

Remembering how I got them

Difficulty in remembering the date and time

I remember two scars that live in my mind

Can't physically see them

Invisible as they may be

These scars haunt me

Not a day goes by that they don't cross my mind

I am wondering

Does it get better with time?

Scars are Forever

Written by George Young

THE PROGRAM

After all these years

My friend changed his mind

The program suggests, living one day at a time

Being the example of the promises of freedom

Attracting newer members, the moment we greet them

Giving hope for a better way

Not having to suffer day to day

Stay vigilante and just do what the old timers say

It works

Living one day at a time

Sadly, my friend changed his mind

Why? I heard his friend's cry

Tears running from their eyes

We did not see this coming

In the end, we all know that this Disease is very cunning

Just live one day at a time

Written by George Young

LOVE CONQUERS ALL

I've been many places

I've met many people

I've learned to respect others

I recognize the differences

Black, Brown, White and Yellow

Creator above

Built this life based on love

Love thy neighbor, love thy friend, love yourself

We all win

Stop the hate, stop the violence

Look around, no more silence

I have a peace sign tattoo on my wrist

Believing love conquers all

That's why we exist

Written by George Young

HOME

There is no place like home

Familiar surroundings

People I recognize

Children who dream of better lives

My eyes have seen young men die

Friends who betray other friends with secrets and lies

Our struggles of the past remain unknown

No knowledge of our kings who stood on the throne

Ignorance has grown

There is so much that we do not know

Why is it so hard to survive in a place we call home

Why can't we share and live as one?

One family, were we all belong

Written by George Young

THINGS CHANGE

Another year has passed

Here we are together again

So much to tell each other

Just where do we begin

The children, how they have grown

Were babies in arms last year

Are running around playing

They are so sweet and dear

Men are so proud

To say this is my wife

What a happy change

She has made in my life

We've had our share of troubles

Everything hasn't been peaches and cream

We've kept our faith in God

He has blessed us to extremes

Let's hope and pray together

That next year we will meet again

There is power in prayer

That God will protect us there

Written by Leona McCoy Young

MY CHILD, MY CHILD

For such a short time, you were mine to cherish and love

God called to you from Heaven above

All I have left now are memories of you

Your laugh, your smile, things you would say or do

Many a tear I'll shed, Many a sleepless night

How I will miss you, but knowing your all right

Your life on earth is over, the life you had with me

For in my Saviors care, you will forever be

Written by Leona McCoy Young

GOD WILL COMFORT YOU

Death comes to everyone

The day, the hour, we do not know

God above knows all things

When from this earth we must go

Some days and many nights

Your pain will linger still

To your heart peace will come

For it is truly God's will

God will comfort you

When a love one from this earth departs

He will lift your spirits high

He will ease your aching heart

There is so much sadness

When we lose someone, we love

We must face reality

Look to our Savior above

Trust, believe and pray

Have faith in our Savior above

He will see you through this tragedy

With his Pure Love

Written by Leona McCoy Young

LOVE

I love this life

Trembling with anticipation

Deep sighs I dream

Caveman instincts are awakened

My desires are on fire

Fighting a battle that wavers

I love this life

Glowing in the eyes of the Creator

I seek to tap into the source

I dare not be fake

Authenticity is a badge of honor

My daily confirmation is to love thyself

My fate is unknown

I do know

In my skin

I am at home

I love this life

Written by George Young

THESE TWO EYES OF MINE

I've seen so very much

With these two eyes of mine

I've seen the pain of others

In drawn faces and sad eyes

That seem to stare

Looking steadily, as if to glare

Seeing and not seeing at all

The things that I have seen

With these two eyes of mine

I've seen the wonderous makings of God

I've seen the grass, the flowers, the hills

The mountains, the trees, and the fields

I've seen expressions of joy, that made me smile

I've seen joy in the face of a child

I've felt tears streaming

Down my face in a steady flow

When things I've seen will no more

No more life when there is death

Just memories of things I've seen

I am so thankful for these two eyes of mine

Written by Leona McCoy Young

FIRE

Fiore, fire, fire

Go shout it from the mountain

We need water

Do not let the mother fuel burn

No more inciting to riot charcoal filled grills

Withhold the rocket fluid that destroys mankind

War, what is it good for?

I say, absolute disaster

Written by George Young

I AM BLESSED

When I awake in the morning

Open my eyes, put my feet on the floor and stand

Look out the window and look to the sky

I am blessed

To open my mouth and speak

Thank you, God

For the wonders you gave to me

My mind so precise and clear

My eyes so I can see

I am blessed

He healed the sick and raised the dead

He made the blind to see

Demons he cast out of man, he gave his life for you and me

I am blessed

To kneel and say a silent prayer

To give him honor and love

To praise his Holy name

Blessings from Heaven above

I am blessed, I am truly blessed

Written by Leona McCoy Young

LOVE STORY

I thought you loved me

Beautiful lies that warmed my heart

Promises of happiness is all I thought

You penetrated my virgin self

Feelings of pleasure is all I felt

Causing my heart to melt, your kind words were all I thought

Never in a million years would we part

Years gone by as I reflect

Broken promises and a lot of not yet

My heart into pieces that a puzzle can't fix

I gave my love to you, I only have regrets

Time goes by

Separation led to divorce

You gave me hell, you gave me no choice

Love faded fast

I've always imagined that our love would last

Disappointment has ruined myself

My pain, my misery was more than enough

Days of sadness filled my past

I finally got the courage to tell you Kiss My Ass

You shattered my soul

I now know

That you never ever Loved me

Written by George Young

THE DARK CLOUD ABOVE

Rain falling from the sky

Into water below

Coming from Heaven up high

Little birds upon the water

Playing, dipping their wings

Then they fly away

Only to come again in the spring

The beauty of it all

The mystery as to why

The birds can fly

I wonder why can't I?

Of course, I have no wings

What a desire

I wonder why birds fly?

Why can't I?

Written by Leona McCoy Young

LOVING YOU

Honey loving you is wonderful

Loving you is so grand

I am proud to be your woman

Proud that you're my man

There may have been others

That you thought you loved

Loving me was made in Heaven above

Now our joys will be together

Our worries just one

Our life together has just begun

Honey loving you is so wonderful

Loving you is so grand

I am proud to be your woman

Proud that you're my man

Written by Leona McCoy Young

TREE ROOTS

Roots of trees, large and small

Oak trees, Pine, came them all

Without those roots they would fall

There would be no trees at all

Summer spring winter and fall

The trees grow getting so tall

Makes a shadow on a wall

Some are short, some are tall

Written by Leona McCoy Young

OLGA

Watching you leave

Feelings that I don't know how to discuss

Thoughts in my head, I can't trust

Your day is now

Sadness mixed with joy

You leaving has left me with a void

I will miss you

You deserve a fresh start

Your smart, your beautiful

I love your smile

Thinking of time without you

It will hurt for a while

Watching you leave

I will grieve some

I will remember the fun

We shared our inner most thoughts

Watching you leave, just leaves me a little crushed

Written by George Young

SEASONS

There are twelve months in a year

With four different seasons

Spring, Summer, Autumn and Winter

I wonder what's the reason

Summer is very hot

Autumn is the best of all

Winter is cold, snowy and icy

Be careful or you will fall

Written by Leona McCoy Young

GOOD EATING

When I want some home cooked food

I know where to go and eat

I thought I could cook hominy grits

I believe you've got me beat

I ate quite a bit, I know

So, did everyone there

Everything was very good

It couldn't be beat anywhere

You can cook, you can burn

It pleased me to a T

I'll eat your cooking anytime

Everything was okay with me

I'll be back sometime soon

It won't be just to eat

I enjoyed every mo0ment

It certainly was a treat

Written by Leona McCoy Young

CRY FOR HELP

My soul is shattered

You control my every decision

Your power over me has beaten me into submission

I only want to get well

My everyday existence is filled with hell

I want relief from my pain

Everyday abuse is driving me insane

I just can't stop this using thing

I no longer know who I am

My soul is shattered

All that matters

Is that you help me

Written by George Young

I CRY FREEDOM

Marching in picket lines

Holding protest signs

United we stood

In every neighborhood

Voices of the past

Shouting free at last, free at last

I cry freedom

Pain in my heart

Pain in my soul

Memories flooding my mind

That I just can't let go

I remember when we as a people had one common goal

United we stand

Divided we fall

I remember when we stood tall

Say it loud, black and proud

That was our theme song

I cry freedom

Free from dying young

No more mothers losing sons

Education instead of incarceration

Break the chains of discrimination

Improve the lines of communication

Let love and peace serve as our salvation written by George Young p 74

WAGERING A WAR AGAINST FATHER TIME

I am looking in the mirror

There I see lines

Specs of gray

Has me thinking, how can I make them go away

I am aging fast, looking for remedies that will return me

To the image of my past

My body aches

Don't know why

It happens in the morning when I wake

This war, eats at my mind

I am forgetting

Daily thoughts of when it's my time

I am afraid to tell anyone of my struggles

Given out too much information, just might cause me trouble

Wagering a war against Father Time

Don't know if I can win, but

I will die trying

REFLECTION

I'm siting alone in the dark

My thoughts are all over the place

thinking about my life

Where I've been

Where I'm going to end up

These are my thoughts

I'm just trying to figure it all out

I'm alone sitting in the dark

Reflecting

Written by George Young

In this ever-evolving nature of friendship

I shall be true to thyself

Exercising the right to choose the percentage of truth

Honestly in which at any moment can jump off of the tallest skyscraper

My obligations veer from side to side

Freeing myself by placing emotions in snow blizzard conditions

Conditions that require defrosting to understand

Understanding that friendship is sometimes complicated

FREEDOM TRAIN

I woke up riding the Freedom Train

I heard the conductor say we will be reaching our destination

In the next day, excited with emotion

Martin's true words spoken

The Dream has reached the mountain top

I think we finally made it

I fall asleep and wake up

I hear the Conductor announce that here has been a delay

We are experiencing difficulties

Her walks the aisle answering questions

Vague answers he provided

A stern look of worry on his face

He states that we are waiting to be rescued

One passenger shout, rescued from what?

Conductor states that we are in need of many repairs

We just can't move forward

We have all the supplies but we can't quite put them in the right

Working order, to get us going

We have Marcus Vision, Martin's Dream, Malcolm's Rhetoric, Ali Swagger

Thurgood's Intelligence and Obama's Victory but,

We are lacking God's Compassion and Love for one another

We have moved from traitors in the tribe

To dirty ships sailing

Auctions that sold our pure existence to others who could afford to buy

Landed on plantations with crops like cotton

Trees with ropes

Lashes from whips

Tongues cut

Roots deprived

Houses divided and sold regularly

Witnessed speakers like Willie Lynch

Woke up to a Crack and Fentanyl Epidemic

That fuels Black on Black violence

Reasons that we fall short of our destination

I awoke to open my eyes

I see many reasons for the delay

Repairs are desperately needed to move forward

My question in my head

When and how do we make the repairs?

I am still riding the Freedom Train

Written by George Young

OBITUARY

My dearest friend, Heroin, who was also known as Fentanyl died
Suddenly. Heroin was my dearest most loyal friend until I realized that
He was not a friend at all. I suffered bad days with Heroin nagging at my
Soul, He was very convincing to have me believe that he was my only
Love, my only concern, nothing else mattered, it wasn't until my pain
That heroin brought to my life on a repeated basis that I realized that
He was taking me to hell, there were good times that I remember.
My first introduction to Heroin is one that I will always remember.
He had the most beautiful voice, singing to me in sweet whispers,
Telling me that the love is here. Heroin warmed my heart, my soul.
I thought I would never love or need another. I believed every whisper,
I believed that my feelings for Heroin would last forever. I was wrong.
Throughout the duration of my relationship with Heroin, the good times
Were fading. Times were not good at all. I struggled with losing things.
Although Heroin was by my side, everything and everyone seemed to be
Taking a backseat to Heroin. He was a jealous friend, thought that I
Needed no one else. Heroin wanted to be the one constant in my life,
No one or nothing else mattered.
So, I decided to commit Homicide on my dearest most devilish friend.
It was not an easy choice; it was my only choice. My soul, my salvation
Depended on me committing this crime. I am guilty, but justified.
I trust that the court of life will not convict me to suffer any longer,
Release me from Hell. If there is any justice, I will be set free.

Written by George Young

THANK EVERONE

I WOULD LIKE TO GIVE CREDIT TO ALL WHO HAVE CONTRIBUTED TO MAKING POETIC BLOOD RUND DEEP COME ALIVE, WITHOUT THEIR ASSISTANCE, IT WOULD NOT HAVE BEEN AN ENJOYABLE EXPERIENCE TO CREATE. I GIVE SPECIAL THANKS TO AMANDA LINTON-HAMMOND WHO TOOK MY VISION AND PRODUCED THE PERFECT GRAPHIC DESIGN COVER. I LOVE YOU DEARLY. NEXT WOULD-BE YOUTH SPECIALIST DOYU LEE OF THE CHERRYHILL BRANCH OF THE ENOCH PRATT LIBRARY IN BALTIMORE CITY. HIS TECHNICAL EXPERTISE IN ASSISTING ME WITH IMPUTING MY MANUSCRIPT AND COVER TO FIT THE GUIDELINES REQUIRED. HIS NEEDED HELP WAS A BLESSING, WITHOUT HIM I WOULD HAVE BEEN LOST. ALSO, THANKS TO THE ENTIRE STAFF AT THE CHERRYHILL LOCATION OF THE ENOCH PRATT LIBRARY. THEIR SUPPORT AND ENCOURAGEMENT MADE AN ATMOSPEHERE TO STRIVE TO DO MY BEST. A SPECIAL THANK YOU TO MY NIECE MICHELLE RENEE MOODY FOR CONTRIBUTING THE OPENING POEM INTRODUCING POETIC BLOOD RUNS DEEP. LAST BUT NOT LEAST, IS MY COUSIN DANA WHITE, FOR INSPIRING ME TO COME UP WITH THE TITLE AND BRAND FOR MY BOOK.

I LOVE EVERYONE WHO PLAYED A PART IN MAKING THIS BOOK COME TO LIFE. I THANK YOU ALL.